"I hate the fact that your whole future is dictated by how well you do in exams at the ages of 15, 16, 17, 18 on top of hormones & stress, etc."

Beth

Contents

Is this you?

You pay attention in class, do your homework, and study for exams.

But, for some reason, you just don't do well on exams.

Or, maybe you do okay on exams.

But you want to do better.

Or, you get pretty good grades.

But want to get excellent grades.

Whoever "you" are, and at whatever level of education you're in, the short time it takes to read this mini-book will be the start of a whole new "test taking" you.

Nobody likes exams.

I didn't.

And I don't know anyone who does.

But grades do matter.

Getting A's or B's can make a big difference in life.

School is more enjoyable and less stressful.

You feel better about yourself when you do well on exams.

And grades can open or close doors of opportunity.

Excellent grades can mean more choices of colleges to attend.

They can also make a difference when it comes time to apply for a job.

I could go on. But you get the idea.

Imagine this.

You're always relaxed and comfortable when you study for an exam.

You remember most, if not all, of what you study.

You're calm and confident when you take an exam.

You always feel you have plenty of time to complete an exam.

And you always get great grades on exams.

Stop and think about that for a moment.

And let it sink in.

Because that's exactly what you can expect to happen. And soon.

All you'll have to do is spend a few minutes each day reading magical statements called Afformations®.

I'll explain how and why they work later.

But first, an amazing story about a student whose life was changed by Afformations.

The "A student" who wasn't.

Lindsay, a second-year student in a class I taught, was an "A student" in all the important ways:

Came to class every day, eager to learn.

Paid attention. Took part in class discussions.

Completed her assignments on time.

And studied hard for quizzes and exams. But...

No matter how hard she tried, she did poorly on exams.

I had just finished marking a near-failing grade on her mid-term exam when I noticed she had emailed me.

She said she knew she hadn't done well on the exam.

Even though she had studied for hours.

She even attached her written study guide of everything I told the class could be on the exam.

"But," she said, "it always turns out this way."

I met with Lindsay after class and learned she had lost confidence in herself.

She was so frustrated that she kept asking herself questions like "why can't I remember what I study?"

Or "why am I so nervous when I take a test?"

I gave Lindsay six positive questions, called Afformations, to read a few times each day.

Like:

Why do I remember everything I study?"

And "Why do I feel so relaxed and confident when I take an exam?"

All she had to do was read these Afformations a few times a day.

And believe that they would work.

Two weeks later Lindsay came to me after class.

She told me she'd just gotten a grade 15 points higher on a quiz in another class than her best previous grade.

Five weeks later she got a B on her final exam in my class.

Six months later...

Lindsay had transferred to a four-year school and I emailed her to see how she was doing.

I asked if she was still reading her Afformations. And If they were still helping.

"Of course I'm still reading them," she replied. "And I got straight A's on my mid-terms!"

Wow, I thought.

She got straight A's six months after she almost flunked my midterm!

I asked her to write back and tell me more about how often she was reading her Afformations.

And how getting such great grades affected her.

An unexpected surprise.

Lindsay wrote back and told me that when she was a child she was diagnosed with a learning disability called "attention deficit/hyperactivity disorder." (You've probably heard of it by the initials ADHD.)

She described being teased by classmates who called her stupid.

She had no friends—and decided to "just do the very best I can and be satisfied with that."

I thought about how brave and determined she was.

And about how powerful Afformations really are to have worked despite what she was dealing with.

She told me she read the statements every day.

In the morning, during the day, and before going to bed.

"Getting good grades," she said, "gave me so much more confidence in myself."

"I accomplished something
I never thought I could.
I proved to myself I can do
anything I put my mind to!"

Lindsay

Why Afformations worked for Lindsay.

And why they'll work for you:

Noah St. John, the creator of Afformations, understood that our "self-talk"—how we talk to ourselves and to others—affects how we behave.

Example: Let's say you do poorly on exams because you always feel overwhelmed and stressed.

And find yourself thinking, "Why can't I relax when I take an exam?"

Each time you think it or say it, your mind is "programming" that negative belief and reinforcing the behavior you're trying to change.

Computer programmers refer to this process as "garbage in/garbage out."

A usual way to try to change a belief is to repeat a positive statement over and over again until you believe it.

Like: "I'm always relaxed and confident when I take an exam."

But it almost never works because you're trying to convince yourself of something you don't believe.

St. John knew the human mind is always asking questions and looking for the answers.

Questions we ask ourselves.

And questions others ask us.

So, he thought, "Why don't we ask ourselves empowering questions—questions that force us to change our thought patterns from negative to positive to answer them?"

An example of a question with a positive answer would be:

"Why do I always feel relaxed and confident when I take an exam?"

Which is one of the Afformations Lindsay reads each day.

And "why" very soon she was relaxed and confident when she took an exam.

Get started with your Afformations.

Before you read the Afformations on the next page, here's how to get the best—and fastest—results:

1. Choose the Afformations that respond to your negative thoughts or fears.

2. Truly believe they will work—because they will.

3. Carry them with you—in your phone, tablet, or notebook.

4. Read them every day. The more you read them, the sooner they kick in.

5. Read your Afformations with the same emotion you would as if they were already true.

6. And, try writing your own Afformations if it works for you.

Your mind will automatically take care of the rest.

Why am I so relaxed and comfortable
when I study for an exam?

Why am I so focused when I study
for an exam?

Why are my powers of concentration
so strong?

Why do I easily remember what
I study?

Why am I so comfortable and
confident taking an exam?

Why do I always have enough time
to finish an exam?

Why do I always perform up to my
expectations on an exam?

Why does it feel so good to get
excellent grades?

Antonetta's Afformations story.

Antonetta was a bright, confident student who got an A in my class. Someone you knew would succeed at anything she put her mind to.

So imagine my surprise when I got an alarming email from her the next semester at the four-year school in New York she'd transferred to.

"I need your help," she wrote. "I feel overwhelmed in my new surroundings. And I'm losing confidence in my ability to cope."

"I'm also having trouble with a very strict accounting professor who seems annoyed when I ask questions in class. And I'm really afraid I'm going to fail the course."

I wrote some Afformations that addressed her concerns and asked her to stay in touch.

Several weeks later Antonetta reported that things were looking up. She was reading her Afformations each morning on the train to school.

And her mood and grades had improved.

By the time the semester ended, she'd gotten straight A's in all her courses including, she said, "that accounting course with the difficult teacher."

"It's the first time I've ever gotten straight A's. This semester I got a 4.0 GPA.

None of this would have happened without my Afformations.

All my fears and doubts were turned into confidence and belief in myself.

They changed my life."

Antonetta

Isabella's Afformations story.

"Science has always been hard for me.

I was getting poor grades—C's & D's—in earth science.

Going into a test I felt like I just didn't understand the material.

Which would cause me to lose confidence.

Not long after I started reading my Afformations I found myself feeling more comfortable taking a test.

And my test scores were improving.

Then I got a 91 on a quiz a few weeks later!

And by the end of the semester I had boosted my final grade to a B+.

Afformations got me to a level I didn't think I could achieve."

Alex's Afformations story.

Like many students, Alex suffered from anxiety when taking exams. And lacked confidence in the answers he chose.

"I'd find myself changing and erasing my answers because I didn't trust myself to choose the correct ones," he said.

The result was always the same: poor grades and disappointment after hours of studying.

Then he began reading Afformations three or four times a day.

And, in little more than a week, he was amazed when he got an 80 on his first quiz in a new class.

"I always did poorly in the first few exams I took in a new class," he said. "So an 80 was a big break through for me."

Over the next few weeks he got grades of 91, 100, and 95 on three tests in two different classes.

And found himself thinking, "Wow, I did this well"!

By mid-term he was carrying A- averages in both his classes, instead of his typical C- to B-.

"The confidence I got from Afformations proved I was capable of doing much better than I thought I could. And made me a much better student."

More than your grades will change.

You'll feel really good about yourself when your Afformations kick in.

And your grades are rapidly improving.

School will be much more enjoyable.

Not to mention far less stressful.

No more dreading exams.

Anything will seem possible.

Your good grades will create better opportunities.

You may even realize that you're capable of change in other important areas of your life.

Because, the truth is, there are no limits to what you can achieve.

It's all part of the new you.

Thanks to the power of Afformations.

Share your success.

If this book changed your life, please take a moment to leave a review on the book's website or on Amazon. Even if it's just a few words.

Reviews are important because they can help me reach as many students like you as possible.

Finally, share your success with your friends and others, especially on social media.

It's your chance to make a difference in someone else's life.

Pioneers in the history of thought and change.

Noah St. John, the inventor of Afformations

Noah St. John's discovery of Afformations is part of a long history in the exploration of thought and how the mind "creates" the lives we live and can determine our fate.

Emile Coue (1857-1926)

Coue was a French pharmacist who believed that thoughts held by the human mind could influence the physical body.

He proved it with an experiment. Patients to whom he spoke positively about medicine they were taking experienced noticeable improvement.

Patients to whom he said nothing, on the other hand, experienced little, or no, improvement.

New Thought Movement

The New Thought Movement began in the United States in the 19th century.

It promoted the ideas that infinite intelligence, or God, is everywhere. Including inside us.

And we can use that God-power to become better people.

Thoughts are Things, Prentice Mulford - 1889

Mulford, a founder of the Movement, offered a distinction between two "minds."

The "lower material mind" that perceives reality through the physical senses.

And the "higher spiritual mind" that connects us to our divine creator and universal knowledge.

He was first to use the term "law of attraction" to describe the connection between the thoughts that preoccupy our minds and the outcomes they create.

James Allen, "As a Man Thinketh" – 1903

"The body is the servant of the mind." So said Allen, who advocated being aware of, and taking responsibility for, our thoughts.

Napoleon Hill, "Think & Grow Rich" – 1937

Hill's book explained the drive, determination and willpower it took to be successful—personally and financially—based on numerous interviews with titans of business like Andrew Carnegie, Henry Ford, Thomas Edison and many others.

A disciple of the New Thought Movement could have written this memorable statement for which Hills' book is remembered: "Whatever the mind can conceive and believe it can achieve."

Hill's book has sold more than 70 million copies.

Norman Vincent Peale, "Power of Positive Thinking" - 1952

Peale was a minister who was influenced by Napoleon Hill's emphasis on positive thought as part of his "Secret of Success."

Peale's book used numerous anecdotes and testimonials from lay people and experts attesting to how lives were changed as a result of replacing negative thoughts with faith and positive optimism.

Earle Nightingale, "The Strangest Secret" - 1956

Nightingale, known as the Dean of Personal Development, was also inspired by Napolean Hill's "Think and Grow Rich."

He turned six words in Hill's book—"we become what we think about"—into his own best-selling book—and later a video, called "The Strangest Secret."

The strangest secret was that "we become what we think about most of the time."

Thanks to his gift for communicating in simple and powerful ways, "The Strangest Secret" became—and still is—one of the great motivational books of all time.

And the video can still be seen on YouTube.

Dr. Candace Pert, "Molecules of Emotion" - 1997

Dr. Pert, a world renowned neuro-pharmacologist, came to the stunning revelation that "your body is your subconscious mind."

She did so after observing how emotions could trigger the release of peptide—a protein—in the body's organs, tissues, glands, and cells.

Which left physical "memory" of the emotion in the body.

Dr. Pert concluded that memory is stored in many places in the body, not just, or even primarily, in the brain.

Her stated conclusion was "your body is your subconscious mind."

Dr. Bruce Lipton, "The Biology of Belief" - 2005

Dr. Lipton is a biologist whose research on how the human cells function refuted the long-standing belief that our genes alone control our life.

He found that each cell in the body has an outer layer that collects information from the body's environment, including thoughts and beliefs.

And, as a result, it changes how genes function.

This was further proof of what Dr. Pert found in her studies: that there's a direct interaction between mind and body.

"Whether you think you can
or think you can't, you're right."

Henry Ford

Made in the USA
San Bernardino, CA
14 March 2018